WHY

THE
COMMON
GOOD

DO WE HAVE TO PAY ATTENTION IN CLASS?

MELISSA RAÉ SHOFNER

PowerKiDS press.
New York

Published in 2019 by The Rosen Publishing Group, Inc.
29 East 21st Street, New York, NY 10010

First Edition

Editor: Jennifer Lombardo
Book Design: Tanya Dellaccio

Photo Credits: Cover Tom Wang/Shutterstock.com; p. 5 Monkey Business Images/Shutterstock.com; pp. 7, 22 SunKids/Shutterstock.com; p. 9 Asia Images Group/Shutterstock.com; p. 11 goodluz/Shutterstock.com; p. 13 India Picture/Shutterstock.com; p. 15 OJO Images/Getty Images; p. 17 iofoto/Shutterstock.com; p. 19 Brian Summers/First Light/Getty Images; p. 21 wavebreakmedia/Shutterstock.com.

Cataloging-in-Publication Data

Names: Shofner, Melissa Raé.
Title: Why do we have to pay attention in class? / Melissa Raé Shofner.
Description: New York : PowerKids Press, 2019. | Series: The common good | Includes index.
Identifiers: LCCN ISBN 9781538330807 (pbk.) | ISBN 9781538330791 (library bound) | ISBN 9781538330814 (6 pack)
Subjects: LCSH: Attention–Study and teaching–Juvenile literature. | Listening–Study and teaching–Juvenile literature. | Study skills–Juvenile literature.
Classification: LCC LB1065.S56 2019 | DDC 370.15'23–dc23

Manufactured in the United States of America

CPSIA Compliance Information: Batch #CS18PK: For Further Information contact Rosen Publishing, New York, New York at 1-800-237-9932

CONTENTS

Good for the Community

A group of people who live or work in the same place is called a community. Community members often care about the same things. People can belong to many communities, such as their family and neighborhood. You probably spend a lot of time at school. Your school is a community, too!

When people work toward the common good, they're doing something that **benefits** their whole community. This shows they care about themselves and others. It also makes people happy and keeps a community running smoothly. One of the best ways to **contribute** to the common good at school is by paying attention in class.

Ready to Learn

A classroom is a smaller community inside the larger school community. You and your classmates go to school each day to learn. Your teacher is there to teach you about important subjects such as history and math. When you pay attention in class, you learn important information better.

Paying attention in class is good for everyone in your classroom. It shows respect for your classmates, who are also trying to pay attention and learn. It also shows respect for your teacher, who is sharing knowledge with you. You can set a good example for others by paying attention in class.

Don't Be a Distraction

There are many reasons students sometimes don't pay attention in class. You may find the **lesson** boring, or you might find something else in the class more interesting. Things that take your attention away from learning are called distractions. Even feeling tired or hungry can be a distraction.

You can help your classmates by not being a distraction. It's hard for other students to learn if you're doing something that distracts them, such as yelling out answers or playing with toys you shouldn't have in class. When you're a distraction, it shows you don't care that your classmates are trying to learn. It can also get you in trouble.

Testing Your Knowledge

Teachers give homework and **tests** to see what their students have learned. They may also ask students questions during class to see if they're paying attention. It's easier to get good grades on homework and tests if you pay attention in class. Your classmates will also get better grades without distractions.

17

Your teacher probably spends much of the day talking to your class. If you pay attention, your teacher won't need to **repeat** things they've already said. You'll understand directions better and be able to do your work the right way. You might even be able to help another student who has a question.

The Classroom Common Good

When you pay attention, you'll know if you don't understand part of the lesson. You'll be able to ask better questions, which helps you and your classmates learn better. Paying attention is one of the best and easiest ways to contribute to the common good of your classroom.

If you're having trouble paying attention in class, you should talk to your teacher. You may need to sit somewhere else so you're not distracted. Be sure to eat a good breakfast and get enough sleep so you're ready to learn. Everyone in your classroom benefits when you pay attention in class.

GLOSSARY

benefit: To be helpful or useful to.

contribute: To give something, such as goods, money, or time, to help another person, group, or cause.

lesson: An activity or class in which you learn something.

repeat: To make, do, or say something again.

test: A set of problems or questions that measure a person's knowledge and skills.

INDEX

WEBSITES

Due to the changing nature of Internet links, PowerKids Press has developed an online list of websites related to the subject of this book. This site is updated regularly. Please use this link to access the list: www.powerkidslinks.com/comg/attn